RUTH BRECKMAN had a career in the travel industry for twenty years. Her dream was to become a travel writer. This has been fulfilled with her first book.

Ruth lives in north London with her husband. She has two daughters and two grandchildren.

Selected Opera Houses
for Everyone Around the World

Selected Opera Houses
for Everyone Around the World

Ruth Breckman

ATHENA PRESS
LONDON

SELECTED OPERA HOUSES FOR EVERYONE AROUND THE WORLD
Copyright © Ruth Breckman 2008

All Rights Reserved

ISBN: 978 1 84748 249 5

First published 2008 by
ATHENA PRESS
Queen's House, 2 Holly Road
Twickenham TW1 4EG
United Kingdom

Printed for Athena Press

Contents

Part Four: The United States of America

Part Five: South America

Part Six: The Far East

Part Seven: Australia

Acknowledgements

I greatly appreciate my husband, Samuel G, for accompanying me to the opera houses.

I am grateful to my daughter, Amanda, for her advice and support throughout.

Thank you for the encouragement given to me from my daughter, Michelle.

Introduction

Opera and ballet are often seen as elitist pastimes, aimed at a select group of people who can afford to go to the theatre regularly and be entertained. But, the magnificent opera houses around the world open their doors for everyone.

Three operatic tenors – Placido Domingo, José Carreras and Luciano Pavarotti – sang together in concerts around the world from the 1990s, performing arias in sport stadiums and large outdoor venues. Known collectively as 'The Three Tenors', they attracted ecstatic pop and opera fans of all ages. Their signature tunes – 'Nessun Dorma' from Puccini's *Turandot* and the Italian ballad 'O Sole Mio' – are best-selling recordings and can be heard in shops and restaurants, proving opera can be enjoyed by everyone!

Visiting opera houses on my travels has inspired me to write an easy-to-use and concise travel companion for tourists of all ages and backgrounds. Every opera house is unique in its architecture, history, seasons, ticket prices and fascinating tours.

I hope this book will give travellers the enjoyment and excitement that have I experienced when visiting these distinct places, as well as give a glimpse of the lighter side of this age-old art form.

My journey takes us from London to Sydney.

Part One

United Kingdom

Royal Opera House
Covent Garden
London

*T*he Royal Opera House in Covent Garden welcomes thousands of visitors each year, with daytime opening to the public since 1999. The opera house has many individual spaces which are used for various events. One such popular venue, particularly for free jazz concerts, is the Paul Hamlyn Hall. 'In Conversation' events with artists and directors are also held at the opera house, in various rooms. Originally a part of the old flower market in Covent Garden, it has become a modern gathering place for everyone and hosts many events, such as tea dances. The Amphitheatre Terrace has rooftop views overlooking this hall and Covent Garden.

The building is the home of the Royal Opera, Royal Ballet and the orchestra of the Royal Opera House. The façade, foyer and grand auditorium date from 1858, when the third theatre, designed by Edward Barry Middleton, was built on the site. This theatre became the Royal Opera House in 1892.

There are four tiers in the theatre – the stalls circle, the Donald Gordon grand tier, balcony and the Amphitheatre. The orchestra stalls are on ground level and the lower and upper slips are on the highest level, and not suitable for children. There are many spacious boxes in the grand tier and the balcony. The Royal Opera House has a capacity for 2,268 people, including 108 standing in various areas. Soft lighting consists of small, red, pleated lampshades perched on gold-plated fittings, which surround the horseshoe-shaped auditorium. The stage has a plush, red velvet curtain trimmed with gold braid and fringes. The main auditorium is a Grade I listed building.

The Royal Opera celebrated its 60th anniversary in 2007 with an exhibition of various memorabilia in the Amphitheatre Bar. Likewise, the Royal Ballet enjoyed its 75th birthday in 2006. The ballet has links with other top companies such as the Russian Kirov Ballet and the Paris Ballet. Works by founder choreographer, Sir Kenneth MacMillan, are regularly performed.

The opera and ballet season runs from September to July, and all opera productions are sung in the original language with English surtitles projected.

The London Coliseum

The London Coliseum is home to the English National Opera (ENO) and all its productions are sung in English. The ENO performs a variety of works, from the classics to Gilbert and Sullivan and new experimental works. They present a repertory of productions on selected nights in the week for the majority of the year. At certain times in the year, the ENO hands over the theatre to major dance companies, which include the English National Ballet and the Bolshoi Ballet.

The London Coliseum was styled as the 'People's Palace of Entertainment and Art'. This Italian Renaissance-style theatre is one of the largest in London, with a large external revolving globe supported by eight figures shaped like cupids. This feature can be seen from a far distance. The London Coliseum opened on the 24 December 1904 with a variety bill and was converted to an opera house in 1968. Frank Matcham, a famous London theatre architect, designed the flamboyant building, which is situated in St Martin's Lane. It is a Grade II listed building and accommodates 2,358 people.

The auditorium is built on four levels: stalls, dress circle, grand tier and balcony. It gives the illusion of a Roman arena, with circular surroundings decorated with white and gold faces, despite the fact that the room is square. The splendid Edwardian interior houses the capital's largest stage, framed by heavy, purple curtains. In 2003, the original glass roof was restored. A two-storey lobby and bar have glorious views of Trafalgar Square.

Backstage tours are available and can include a visit to the Royal Box, the balcony, the orchestra's pit and, on certain occasions a glimpse of behind the scenes.

Opera House Boscombe Dorset

This magnificent Victorian opera house is located within a bustling shopping precinct in the centre of the Boscombe town. The historic theatre has been owned by Mr John Butterworth's family since April 1944 and it is one of very few independently owned opera houses left in the United Kingdom.

On 27 May 1895, the grand opening of the Opera House, known at that time as the Boscombe Grand Theatre, comprised musical, comedy and drama productions, grand opera and an indoor circus. The cages used for elephant and tiger acts were kept in the basement after having been transported through 30 ft tunnels from King's Park! The architect was Archibald Beckett and the theatre was built as part of an imposing development that included The Royal Arcade.

The opera house became known as the Boscombe Hippodrome in 1905 and featured regular appearances from talented music hall artists. In the 1930s and 1940s, comedians Laurel and Hardy, Tommy Trinder and Flanagan and Allen entertained audiences at the Hippodrome. In 1944, Irving Berlin played 'This Is The Army'.

The dancing and music scene of the late 1950s brought further success when the opera house reopened as the Royal Arcade Ballrooms in 1956. Rock 'n' roll stars Pink Floyd performed in 1968, as did Led Zeppelin and David Bowie in 1972.

Many changes occurred in 1982, when the opera house reopened again, this time called Academy Nightclub, and was the venue for popular acts such as Frankie Goes To Hollywood. Since January 1997, the theatre has been known as the Opera House and has been used for modern music and dancing.

The Grade II listed building was reopened on 1 June 2007 having undergone striking renovations to its exquisite interior by Oates construction. A modern LED lighting system has been installed to create an exciting atmosphere, with every corner of the house being touched by the sixteen million colour permutations. Twenty-first-century technology, lighting and sound are combined with the traditional elegance and grandeur of the theatre from a bygone age.

The ornate horseshoe auditorium is lined with slender pillars, decorated with gold leaves. The gold-and-white proscenium arch on the front of the huge stage has a facial mask above the centre and dramatic, heavy, black curtains framing it. An intricate, wrought-iron verandah overlooks the auditorium from the dress circle.

With the refurbishment, the 'gods' have been opened for the first time in seventy years. Originally, the servants occupied the seats up in the 'gods', with a separate exit leading to an alleyway into the streets. Now open to all, the original Victorian seating has also been refurbished.

James Brennan, the opera house events producer, tells some fascinating tales of ghost stories. Security guards have seen images of clowns in the gallery, strange shadows and weird sounds of footsteps up in the 'gods'.

The gallery on the first floor is suitable for small functions. It is decorated with colourful stained-glass windows and black-and-white graffiti-style pictures of jazz musicians. Visitors to the opera house can meet at the pre-show bar in the gallery.

Every floor has black granite art deco style drinking bars, imported from Italy by the interior designer Stuart Jones.

There are twelve private booths for six or ten people and two royal boxes for corporate and private hire with a fully stocked private bar and a VIP entrance to view the shows. This superb opera house seats 800 people or 1,800 people standing.

All year round this amazing venue is used for comedy, live music and various forms of cabaret-style evenings. The Opera House in Boscombe brings social and cultural events to the south coast.

Part Two

Europe

Opéra National de Paris Garnier

Paris
France

The opulent Opéra de Paris Garnier, also known as Opéra Garnier, was designed by Charles Garnier for Emperor Napoleon III. He was the winner of an open architectural competition, chosen for his decorative style and planned use of stone, marble and bronze. The Opéra de Paris Garnier is considered to be grander and more elaborately decorated than any of its European contemporaries. It is a prime example of 19th century neo-Baroque style. It is located on Avenue de l'Opéra, where it was deliberately kept free of trees so as not to mask the wonderful views of the magnificent building.

The majestic Opéra Garnier is now home to the Ballet de l'Opéra de Paris. This internationally renowned ballet company is headed by dance director Brigitte Lefèvre and boasts an extensive repertoire including romantic, classic and contemporary dance. The dance season runs from mid-September until the end of June.

Construction of the Opéra Garnier began in 1862, but it was not completed until 1875, partly because an underground lake was discovered. The small lake was the secret hiding place of the phantom of the opera in Gaston Leroux's haunting play.

It has a spectacular and extravagant façade that is divided into separate white, pink and green marble colonnades. It is also adorned with rearing horses, winged angels and gleaming gold busts of composers. The beautiful building is magically illuminated on performance nights.

The magnificent grand staircase (Escalier d'Honneur) is made out of imported multi-coloured marble. The staircase is 30 m (98 ft) high. The grand foyer is superb, with a domed ceiling covered in mosaics and a large number of sparkling crystal chandeliers. High-society ladies in shimmering gowns of years gone by used the foyer as a place to meet and be seen during the interval.

The five-tiered auditorium is covered in red velvet, plaster cherubs and gold leaves. Either side of the auditorium's entrance stands a bronze statue – one depicting comedy and the other depicting tragedy.

In 1964, Marc Chagall created a large painting on the interior ceiling. His work depicted Paris landmarks and colourful scenes from operas and ballets.

On the side of the Opéra Garnier building, facing Rue Scribe, is the Pavilion d'Honneur, a small but delightful museum. It contains photographs of famous artists, models of stage sets and busts of major composers. The ballet shoes of the Russian dancer, Waslow Nijinsky, and tarot cards bring nostalgia to the atmosphere. Theatre scripts, musical scores and dancing memorabilia are also enjoyable to browse through on your visit.

Teatro alla Scala
Milan
Italy

*T*eatro alla Scala established Milan as the opera capital of the world. In Italy, opera is popular with all ages and all classes of Italians, who consider it to be their national music.

The Teatro alla Scala was founded by Empress Maria Theresa of Austria to replace the Royal Ducal Theatre, which was destroyed by fire on 26 February 1776 and which, until then, had been the home of opera in Milan.

More commonly known as La Scala, it was built by Guiseppe Piermarini in 1778. It was originally illuminated with oil lamps and, to alleviate the risk of fire, several rooms were filled with hundreds of buckets of water. In time, oil lamps were replaced by gas lamps and these, in turn, were substituted with electric lights in 1883.

In 1943, during World War II, La Scala was severely damaged by bombing. It was rebuilt and reopened on 11 May 1946. The theatre closed in 2002 for renovation, with the beginning of a new reconstruction project. Only the neoclassical style façade remained standing, and the renovation was completed on 7 December 2004.

The traditional gala opening night of the opera season is

7 December. The opera season runs from January until July, and from September until November, overlapping with the ballet season. In December, La Scala hosts symphonic concerts with the Philharmonic Orchestra (Filarmonica della Scala).

The interior of La Scala appears smaller than other European opera houses, but the seating capacity is 2,800. The intimate auditorium has four tiers of red velvet boxes and detailed red-and-gold decor. The central royal box looks out on a magnificent, gleaming chandelier, further creating an opulent atmosphere.

The stage is one of the largest stages in Italy, measuring 1,200 sq m (13,000 sq ft), and is framed by a heavy, red, velvet curtain, trimmed with gold braid. There is a spacious foyer lined with large mirrors, Carrara marble and elaborate Bohemian crystal chandeliers.

Teatro alla Scala is also home to the Theatre Museum, Museo Teatrale alla Scala, officially inaugurated in 1913. The museum is an interesting attraction for theatre lovers. It houses portraits, instruments, mementoes of opera and ballet stars of the past, and souvenirs of the opera house alongside costumes worn by Maria Callas, Carla Fracci, and Rudolf Nureyev.

In 1901, Verdi died in a Milan hotel. His immaculate desk is an exhibit at the museum along with his original notepaper, playing cards and a French dictionary.

Guided tours of the Ansaldo Workshops are exciting and allow the backstage workings of every production at the Teatro alla Scala to be explored. The tour takes visitors through all of the pavilions and offers the tourist an opportunity to see joiners, blacksmiths, carpenters, dressmakers and costume designers at work.

Arena di Verona
Verona
Italy

*I*taly's best-preserved Roman arena, Arena di Verona, was once home to the spectacle of feeding Christians to the lions. Looking in to the enormous ring, it is easy to imagine gladiators fighting for their lives. The Roman amphitheatre was built at the beginning of the 1st century to fulfil the demand of the Roman people for gymnastic competitions and hunting games.

In August 1913, an audience gathered to hear an opera performance of *Aida*, and the event was a great success. Since then, crowds have come every summer to hear some of the world's finest artists and musicians perform opera, ballet and contemporary music.

The interior of the massive arena is impressive. From the pit, there is flight upon flight of giant terraces, which sweep upwards in ever-widening circles. The stage floor is the largest in Europe at approximately 44 m (145 ft) by 26 m (86 ft). The arena originally accommodated 20,000 people, but now holds around 15,000. Unusual stage props are utilised, which are suited to the grand scale of the arena.

The structure of the Roman amphitheatre is composed of concrete and rubble, with an outer ring of brick and stone quarried from the hills around Verona. This combination of materials produces an attractive colour contrast. Nearly the whole of the perimeter wall of the building has disappeared; all that remains today is the 'Ala' (wing), which towers above the arena. It is composed of three tiers with four arches remaining on each tier, and it is the only part remaining from the original façade.

Seating around the inside is on forty-five rows made of marble, so it is advisable to bring something soft to sit on! The stalls section, the '*poltronissime* gold' (first sector stalls, gold), provide the maximum quality in sound and vision. The reserved seats will be the most central and the nearest to the stage. Seating in the arena consists of unreserved stone steps, numbered seats on the step (in the centre), lateral numbered seats on the step (cheaper and on the sides), second sector stalls and first sector stalls.

The opera season in the Roman amphitheatre runs from June until September. Performances do not begin until sunset and the surrounding candlelit area becomes part of the stage. In Verona, opera is regarded as popular entertainment and is not something reserved only for highbrow audiences. The arena is the city's crowning glory; it has survived the passage of time, always holding an important position in the public and cultural life of Verona.

Die Wiener Staatsoper

Vienna

Austria

A grand entrance hall with a majestic staircase is a fitting introduction to an evening of classical music at the Staatsoper (Vienna State Opera). Vienna Staatsoper sets the highest standards of top international performers, producers and set designers. The Vienna State Opera is closely connected to the Vienna Philharmonic Orchestra. Performances are given 300 days a year: fifty operas and twenty ballets.

Once a year, on the last Thursday of *fasching* (carnival), the stage and stalls of Staatsoper are transformed into one gigantic dance floor. The hall is covered in fresh flowers, and this is the glorious scene of the most glittering event of the season: the Vienna Opera Ball.

The Staatsoper was built between 1860 and 1869, with a Renaissance arched-style façade designed by August von Siccardsburg and Edward van der Null. Over the main façade, there are imposing riders on two flying horses, representing harmony and the muse of poetry, designed by Ernst Julius Hähnel. In the arches of the open-sided *loggia* are five bronze statues which portray heroism, the songstress, fantasy, Thalia (the

Greek goddess and muse of comedy and poetry) and love.

At the front of the Staatsoper are two old fountains by Josef Gasser that represent opposing worlds, namely music, dance, joy and light-heartedness opposing grief, love and revenge.

Originally, the opera house was called Hofoperntheater (Vienna Court Opera). Emperor Franz Joseph once criticised the theatre, saying it looked like a railway station. During World War II, the building and the stage were destroyed by fire on 12 March 1945. However, the entire façade, central stairway, the entrance *loggia* and tea room remained intact. The elaborate foyer with superb frescoes by Moritz Von Schwind, including the painted cycle of Mozart's *Magic Flute*, were saved. The painter's valuable work is now protected with a glass covering which remains in place from November until April each year.

Erich Boltenstern rebuilt the new opera house using unique plans. The auditorium was maintained from the 1869 design of three box circles and two open circles, with seating for 2,200 people. A new safety curtain decorated with a picture of Orpheus and Eurydice rose on 5 November 1955 with a performance of Beethoven's *Fidelio*.

The Staatsoper has three different roof shapes. The vaulted roof surrounds the higher, central parts of the building, covering the auditorium and the stage. The roof on the second storey links between the lateral wings and there is a French roof on the corner turrets.

Music lovers can also revive memories of past perform- ances at the new Vienna State Opera Museum. The focus is upon the period between 1955 and 2005, since the opera house's reopening. Here, visitors can walk clockwise through the fifty years of its opera history.

Part Three

Eastern Europe

Hungarian State Opera House

Budapest
Hungary

*J*n 1873, a competition for a new theatre design in Budapest was won by Miklos Ybl, a Hungarian architect trained in Vienna. Emperor Franz Joseph of the Austro-Hungarian Empire financed the elaborate construction. The superb neo-Renaissance and neo-Baroque style of the Hungarian State Opera House (Magyar Állami Operház) was completed in September 1884. The opening show, Erkel's *Bánk Bán* was a huge success.

Miklos Ybl created a replica of the *loggia* of the Paris Garnier, the ground foyer and impressive marble staircase from Vienna and he also adopted the neo-Renaissance decoration of Dresden. On the stately façade, Ybl mixed all these influences in order to create his own personal style.

The statues on the façade, renovated in 1966, represent several great composers: Monteverdi, Scarlatti, Gluck, Mozart, Beethoven, Rossini, Donizetti, Glinka, Wagner, Verdi, Gounod, Bizet, Moussorgsky, Tchaikovsky, Moniuszko and Smetana.

The interior of the opera house is amazing. In the entrance there are statues of Franz Liszt, who founded the Franz Liszt Academy of Music, and Ferenc Erkel, who wrote the Hungarian national anthem and was the first musical director of the opera. There is also an extravagant, dominant chandelier.

The ceiling frescoes were painted by Károly Lotz and the spectacular paintings on the walls are by the Hungarian masters, Bertalan Szekely and Mor Than. The upstairs reception rooms are lavish, decorated with portraits and busts of Hungarian divas and composers.

The auditorium has three tiers of boxes, one top gallery and a seating capacity of 1,600. It was the first in Europe to feature a safety curtain (installed after the fire at the Vienna Opera House), an all-metal stage hydraulics sprinkler system, under-floor heating and air conditioning. The box used by Emperor Franz Joseph's wife Sissi, who loved the Hungarian opera, is positioned to the left of the stage.

The Hungarian State Opera House was once the most modern theatre in the world. It was reopened after reconstruction in 1984 – the year of its centenary.

The Hungarian State Opera and the Hungarian State Ballet share the stage and present over fifty major productions, many of which will be familiar to foreign opera lovers. The main season at the opera house lasts from September to the middle of June. A prestigious opera ball is held annually in February at the Hungarian State Opera.

It is one of the city's most historic buildings and Budapest residents are proud of this important tourist attraction.

The Prague State Opera
National Theatre and
Estates Theatre
Prague, Czech Republic

There are three opera houses in Prague: the Prague State Opera (Státní opera Praha), the National Theatre and the Estates Theatre. Each opera house has a unique architectural and cultural appeal. They present a rich repertoire of opera, ballet and classical concerts.

There is a choice of major new productions each year, presented in their original languages. Sometimes, English and Czech surtitles are provided. An evening at the opera is, for many visitors, a highlight of their trip to Prague.

The Prague State Opera is situated at the top of Wenceslas Square and is close to the National Museum. This impressive neo-Rococo building has an interior of lavish gold and red furnishings.

Originally named the German Theatre, the Prague State Opera opened in 1888 to tremendous welcome from the public. At the end of World War II, as Czechoslovakia became a Communist state, the opera house was known as the Smetana Theatre. It suffered badly from neglect. Performances were few and far between without a prepared programme.

Its renaissance came in 1992, after the fall of

communism, when the name changed back to the Prague State Opera.

Operas are staged every day, mostly in Italian. Verdi is extremely popular in Prague, with an annual Verdi Festival in late August and September. Sometimes, there are variety shows by German and Russian composers.

The Prague State Opera is closed from the end of June until mid-August. At Christmas, the Prague State Opera becomes the grand setting for classical music concerts and on New Year's Eve hosts a celebrated gala evening. Smart dress is required and no jeans allowed!

The National Theatre (Národní Dívadlo) is a cultural institution for the Czech people that has, for several centuries, promoted the development of the Czech language. Prague's finest opera, ballet and drama are performed at the National Theatre. It is located alongside the peaceful Vltava River.

The National Theatre represents the Czech people in the 19th century. It was paid for with enthusiasm by public subscription. The first performance of Smetana's opera, *Libuše*, was held at the official opening on 11 June 1881. Sadly, shortly afterwards, the theatre was totally destroyed after workers accidentally set fire to the building.

Two years later, a new house was completed by Josef Schulz (also the designer of the National Museum) who adopted his mentor, Josef Zitek's, original plan. The inscription at the entrance declares, 'Narod Sobe', meaning, 'the nation's [gift] to itself'.

A distinctive golden roof can be seen from a far distance. There are two dramatic bucking horses on the gold dome of this neo-Renaissance building. The five arcades of the open *loggia* are decorated with paintings by Josef Tulka entitled, 'Five songs'.

The extravagant interior decoration, including the

massive ceiling of reds and golds, creates a wonderful atmosphere for a special night in Prague. The auditorium has three tiers of boxes, two balconies and two galleries, with a seating capacity of 1,554.

The former royal box is lined with red velvet and decorated with famous figures from Czech history by Vaclav Brozik.

A controversial extension to the theatre called the 'New Stage' (Nova Scena) was completed in 1983. It was designed by architect Karel Prager. Love it or hate it, with a series of gigantic glass boxes, the New Stage is certainly eye catching!

The National Theatre's abundance of paintings and statues announces the glories of the Czech nation and its people.

The Estates Theatre (Stavovské Divadlo) is one of the oldest and most historical theatres in Europe. Wolfgang Amadeus Mozart is remembered at the Estates Theatre for his dramatic impact on the city of Prague. It was here that he conducted the world premiere of *Don Giovanni* on 29 October 1787. From then on, the theatre's place in musical history was assured.

The Opera Mozart Company stages this opera every summer. The repertoire of the Estates Theatre consists mainly of Mozart's operas. However, other famous composers feature occasionally, as well as ballet productions and classical concerts.

The elegant neoclassical architecture in the Estates Theatre is exceptional; it was built and financed by Count Nostitz in 1783. The auditorium has two tiers of boxes, in dark blue and gold, and a seating capacity of 1,000. The foyer is open for performances only.

Part Four

The United States of America

The Metropolitan
Opera House
New York

*T*he elegant Metropolitan Opera House, home of the Metropolitan Opera, is situated at the centre of the Lincoln Center Plaza in New York City. The Lincoln Center was built in the 1950s on 16.3 acres, transforming slums into a giant cultural complex. The Met was designed by architect Wallace K Harrison, and opened on 16 September 1966, with the world premiere of Samuel Barber's *Anthony and Cleopatra*.

The Metropolitan Opera has been one of the world's leading opera companies since its opening in 1883 at the first Metropolitan Opera House, or 'Old Met', originally located on Broadway. The American Ballet Theatre and many other international artists' groups perform at the Met and consequently, the Met continues to achieve musical and dramatic excellence.

Each season, the Met stages more than 200 performances of opera in New York. This ranges from *Tosca* to *On the Town*, which means that the Metropolitan Opera House appeals to a wide range of people. The season runs from September to early May.

The building is clad in white travertine, and the east

façade has five colourful, tall arched windows, which are clearly visible from the plaza. In the opulent foyer are two magnificent murals created by Marc Chagall, which are protected from the morning sun with a covering.

Exquisite chandeliers are raised to the ceiling before each performance, which is quite extraordinary to see. Red-carpeted staircases were designed in the 1960s to encourage an atmosphere of formal evening wear, but the present-day dress code is smart/casual.

The Met's crimson, velvet, diamond-shaped auditorium has a main curtain of woven gold damask. This curtain is one of the largest curtains in the world. The gold proscenium is 54 ft wide and 54 ft high and the theatre has a seating capacity of 3,800. There are some wonderful views of the plaza from the café at the top of the lobby.

The Metropolitan Opera runs the Lindemann Young Artist Development Program, dedicated to nurturing talented young artists. The Met is equipped with some of the finest technical facilities. All of the productions are translated using their world-renowned 'Met Titles', using computerised screens at every seat in the opera house.

Children of all ages and backgrounds participate in regular programmes organised by the Metropolitan Opera Guild Education Department. They have the opportunity to learn about all aspects of the arts, including music, theatre, dance, and the visual arts as well as history, literature and foreign language.

Backstage tours of the Met are exciting and offer the tourist a chance to go behind the scenes, visiting the stars' dressing rooms and the rehearsal rooms. This offers the chance to see a view of the grand auditorium, the stage complex, enormous sets and beautiful costumes, and is an unforgettable ninety-minute tour.

The Civic Opera House

Chicago

The Civic Opera House is located in the heart of downtown Chicago, on the famous North Wacker Drive. This magnificent opera house is the home of the Lyric Opera of Chicago.

The structure of the imposing building was inspired by Paris' Opera Garnier, shaped like a giant armchair. A combination of art nouveau, French Renaissance and art deco styles, the Civic Opera House is considered to be one of the world's most lavish houses. It was envisioned by Samuel Insull, who was president of the Chicago Civic Opera Association in the 1920s, and has a seating capacity of just over 3,500.

In 1997, a $100 million renovation of the Civic Opera House was completed, both front and backstage.

The fan-shaped solid oak auditorium has thirty-one boxes, orchestra stalls and three balconies. The grand and imposing foyer with gleaming Roman marble floors, Austrian crystal chandeliers, a resplendent staircase and gold leaf-topped marble columns, gives a stately atmosphere of opulence.

Next door to the opera house is The Patrick G and

Shirley W Ryan Opera Center, which also gives fine performances.

The Lyric Opera Company performs various productions, including musicals such as *Sunset Boulevard* and *The Phantom of the Opera*. Special events take place in the season from late September to early March. Once or twice a season, the company performs new avant-garde works by contemporary American composers. Touring classical dance groups fill the off-season bill.

English subtitles make the performances easy to follow, and the opera house has excellent acoustics. The dress code at the Lyric is casual and not at all formal.

Fascinating backstage tours are open to the public in the months of February and March only. Visiting a star's dressing room and hearing stories of how international artists prepare for their performances is not something to be missed if you happen to be in Chicago during these two months.

The Marion Oliver McCaw Hall

Seattle

M arion Oliver McCaw Hall is a performance hall and opera house that captivates the entire community with its striking public promenade and modern luminous design. The Seattle Center is enhanced by the Kreielsheimer Promenade, which was designed by Gustafson Guthrie Nichol. Supporters and guests to the McCaw Hall enjoy gatherings in this outstanding venue.

Within the promenade are a series of glowing, transparent, metal-mesh screens reaching 30 ft high which float ahead and appear to continue into the interior lobby. Three thin sheets of water look like a serpentine glass façade, a water feature which shimmers over sloped paving in the centre portion of the promenade. It reflects the sky and lighting effects at night.

The current hall opened on 28 June 2003, designed by LMN Architects. The work of thirty designers was headed by architect Mark Reddington, interior designer Deborah Sussman, lighting artist Leni Schwendinger and the Seattle Center Director, Virgina Anderson. It was constructed within the steel support structure of the earlier Seattle Opera House, originally created for the World's Fair in 1962.

A donation of $20,000 by saloonkeeper James Osborne in 1881 was added to public funding, but this was insufficient to build the auditorium. David T and Louisa Denny donated land for a new hall in 1886, but the construction was delayed due to the Great Seattle Fire in 1889, the gold rush and World War I. In 1927, a bond measure was approved by Seattle voters and the auditorium was built. It was dedicated by Seattle's only female Mayor, Bertha K Landes.

There are three lobby spaces in the new McCaw Hall: Grand Lobby, First Tier Lobby and Second Tier Lobby. They are designed to be the perfect setting during intermission with dramatic, open spaces. Each lobby is accessible by stairs or elevators.

The hall's shimmering interiors are decorated with 132 bold colours taken from the full palette of the Northern Lights. From watery-grey days to splendid gold-and-red sunsets. The walls change colour as you move around them, in eye-catching contrasts of red, orange and purple.

On the stage, a twenty-four-foot trapdoor divided into multiple sections may be customised for each performance. A motorised curtain on stage can be operated by remote control.

The auditorium has been reconfigured to improve sight-lines, acoustics and create a more intimate relationship between the artists and audience. There are a total of sixteen new boxes – eight on each sidewall – with seats that face the stage not the auditorium. The seating capacity is 2,900 with standing room along the orchestra level.

McCaw Hall obtains some of the best acoustics in the world. With low velocity ducts located underneath the seats, drafts are minimized and temperatures kept more even. There is a 400-seat lecture hall and a Café Impromptu.

The hall is home to Seattle Opera and Pacific Northwest Ballet. The Seattle Opera general director is currently

Speight Jenkins and the Pacific Northwest Ballet artistic co-director is currently Kent Stowell.

The season runs from August to May for opera, and from September to June for ballet. Community festivals and guest performances from around the world, as well as weddings, conventions and receptions are welcome at the state-of-the-art opera house.

Part Five

South America

Teatro Solís
Montevideo
Uruguay

The Teatro Solís opera house is respected as the jewel of the city in the community of Montevideo. This imposing building is located in the old town and the main entrance is on the Buenos Aires street corner, at Bartholomew Mitre, Independence Square.

The façade of the Teatro Solís was designed as an Italian opera house, similar to La Scala in Milan. A restored lamp post is situated on the top of the theatre and it has a red light, which signals when lit that a performance is taking place.

The theatre took fifteen years to build: from 1841 to 1856. A group of shareholders wanted to have an important theatre in Montevideo and to hire it for the benefit of its members.

The inauguration of the Solís Theatre took place on 25 August 1856, with the theatre being named after the Spanish explorer Juan Díaz de Solís, who discovered the Río de la Plata in 1516.

Ermani by Verdi was the first opera to be performed, in the presence of the President of Uruguay Mr Gabriel Antonio Pereira.

The theatre boasts grand marble columns, which have remained untouched since 1856 in the theatre hall, and a sparkling empire-style chandelier. A modern, white-marble staircase leads to the higher levels of the theatre.

The four gallery levels have private boxes and are called Tertulia Baja (low gathering), Tertulia Alta (high gathering), Cazuela and Paraiso (paradise). People can access every level from the main hall. Plush red carpet, comfortable new seats imported from Brazil, air conditioning and new acoustics are many recent improvements to the Teatro Solís.

A dazzling chandelier in the centre of the auditorium lights up the graceful rosette paintings on the ceiling, and the oil paintings around the proscenium arch, decorated with two masks – one Tragedy and one Comedy. In the 1800s, the four boxes to the right of the stage were reserved for wealthy people to show off their affluent status in society and observe the audience. However, the restricted view stopped them from seeing the performance.

A new orchestra pit has now been placed over a movable platform, which allows three different positions for the orchestra to perform in.

Teatro Solís is the home of the Philharmonic Orchestra of Montevideo, Municipal Theatre Company and National Comedy. The opera season runs from August until November and most of the operas are sung in Italian with surtitles in Spanish.

Teatro Amazonas
Manaus
Brazil

*I*n 1885, rich Portuguese barons, benefiting from the rubber boom, started building the Teatro Amazonas, a neoclassical-style opera house. On the outside of the building, the dome is covered with 36,000 decorated ceramic tiles painted with the colours of the national flag. The roadway by the entrance was made of rubber so that carriages arriving late would not create too much disruptive noise.

The Teatro Amazonas was the vision of Jose Fernandez Junior, a member of the House of Representatives, with an ambition of obtaining music and culture for Manaus.

Expensive materials were imported from Europe. Crispin de Amoral, an artist, supervised the design of the interior. The wood used to lay the floors and build the chairs was taken from the Amazon forest. The stone was from Portugal and the Carrara marble for the stairs, statues, columns, mosaics and 198 crystal chandeliers was transported from Venice. Wrought-iron banisters, clocks and murals came from Paris, and the steel walls were ordered from England.

The sprawling city of Manaus is situated on the banks of

the Río Negro, a primary point of entry into the vast jungle. The maintenance of an opera house in these conditions is not easy, but the cultural significance that Teatro Amazonas brings to Manaus means the maintenance is a small price to pay.

During the 20th century Manaus developed into a modern city, with an international airport, improved roads, visiting cruise ships and an active harbour with nightlife and restaurants.

The elegant interior of the opera house was completed after fifteen years, and has a seating capacity of 1,600. Exquisite painted scenes of music, dance, drama and a tribute to the classical composer, Carlos Gomes, adorn the ceiling.

Opera, dance events, popular and classical concerts fill the stage regularly. It is the home of the Brazilian Symphony Orchestra and has a festival of opera, which takes place during April. The season runs during June, July and August.

The theatre was inaugurated on 31 December 1896, with the first performance occurring on 7 January 1897. The first performance was of an Italian opera, *La Gioconda*, by Amilcare Ponchiellli.

Manaus, and consequently the Teatro Amazonas, had a major decline in fortune when rubber plantations started producing in Malaysia in the early twentieth century. However, the Teatro Amazonas has recently been refurbished as Manaus returns to prosperity.

It has been restored four times: in 1929, 1974 and between 1988 and 1990. It was reopened in the presence of tenor Placido Domingo and ballerina Marcia Haydee.

The theatre has a small museum with a rich history. Items on display include building plans, rare porcelains and information on artists who have performed on its stage.

Part Six

The Far East

The Beijing Opera
Based at the Liyuan Theatre
Beijing, China

The Liyuan Theatre is situated inside the magnificent Beijing Jianguo Qianmen Hotel. There are sparkling lights around the entrance of the hotel, which create an atmosphere of gaiety and entertainment.

Inside the Liyuan Theatre, there are rows of tables with small, gilt table lamps trimmed with red, pleated lampshades. The audience are greeted with courtesy upon arriving and are escorted to a table where they may enjoy delicious flavoured snacks and Chinese tea during the opera.

Beijing opera is a form of Chinese opera which arose in the late eighteenth century and became fully developed and recognised by the nineteenth century. The opera was extremely popular in the Qing Dynasty court and has become one of the cultural treasures in China.

Artists from The Beijing Opera perform a wide repertoire of traditional Chinese stories and routines. Their acting is vivid, with vibrant costumes, intricate face paintings and ornamental headdresses.

It is a joy to watch the graceful movements of the skilful performers. Highlights of the productions at the Liyuan Theatre include the swift Chinese acrobatic show, the

Beijing drama, opera or even Chinese Kongfu. On a sparse stage, the Beijing opera utilises the skills of speech, song, dance and combat movements. Subtitles are translated into international languages.

Traditional Chinese colours are painted on the performer's face and denote the personality. Red denotes uprightness and loyalty, white is visible on evil or crafty characters and black represents qualities of soundness and integrity.

The Beijing Opera's musicians are in front of the customary square platform stage. The artists perform from three sides, and the stage has an embossed curtain called a *Shoujiu*. Musicians are visible to the audience on the front part of the stage. Traditionally, Beijing opera is built above the line of sight of the viewers.

Visitors have been allowed to enter the make-up room to see how actors or actresses apply make-up to their faces with such artistic skill. The history of the Beijing opera, including stage photos of well-known artists, costumes, masks and musical instruments are visible in the display hall.

The Liyuan Theatre welcomes everyone to an elegant and comfortable environment, with its superb opera, and martial art performances.

New National
Theatre

Tokyo
Japan

*T*he New National Theatre (Kokuritsu Gekijo) had its
first public performance on 10 October 1997 and it is
the country's first state-owned theatre. This state of the art
cultural complex has three theatres: the Opera House, the
Playhouse and The Pit.

The Opera House performs opera and ballet. The season
runs from October to June. It has a seating capacity of 1,810.
The Playhouse programme includes plays and
contemporary dance and it seats 1,000. The Pit is the
smallest theatre, with an open-style stage for contemporary
performing arts, and holds 440 seats.

The New National Theatre is located in the western side
of the Shinjuku area of Tokyo, near the Imperial Palace.
Originally built in 1983, the theatre incorporates traditional
Japanese architectural motifs in the design of its sloping
roofs, which reflect Japan's oldest and most stylised form of
theatres.

In the horseshoe-shaped auditorium of the Opera
House, the walls and ceilings are covered in thick panels of
wood to provide the ideal acoustics for the singers. The
orchestra pit seats a full 120-person orchestra.

The stage of the Opera House has four different areas: the main stage, a rear stage and left and right wings. This structure – which is standard in European theatre architecture – has been built to suit grand opera. The New National Theatre is Japan's first full-scale theatre for opera and ballet.

Traditional Japanese forms of theatre include kabuki, bunraku and Noh. Kabuki combines acting, singing and dancing. All roles, including female characters, are played by male actors, but actresses are allowed for certain events. Kabuki features highly ornate settings and costumes.

Bunraku is the traditional Japanese form of puppet theatre and originated in the seventeenth century. Lifelike wooden puppets in vivid costumes are skilfully manipulated to act out a story. Three puppeteers are usually required to operate each puppet.

Noh is the oldest of Japan's theatrical arts dating back to the fourteenth century. It is performed on a simply decorated stage with artists synchronising their movements to symbolic music. Actors were the rock stars of feudal Japan and many of the older plays are still performed today.

Productions of new works in the modern tradition involve collaboration with world-renowned choreographers, designers and conductors. The New National Theatre Ballet in Tokyo continues to grow in fame and popularity. They are loved and respected by all who cherish ballet as their chosen form of artistic expression.

Various enterprises take place at the theatre, including training programmes for young artists, theatre hire for other performing arts groups and public performances for children and students.

The three major companies that currently operate at the New National Theatre are Fujiwara Opera, Nihon Opera and the Kyokai Nikkai Opera.

Part Seven

Australia

Sydney Opera House

The impressive Sydney Opera House looks like a cluster of sailing boats moored in Sydney harbour. A Danish architect, Jørn Utzon, the son of a naval engineer, created the design for an international competition in the late 1950s. It was officially opened by Queen Elizabeth II on 20 October 1973.

Monumental granite steps rise up towards the main building from the forecourt and provide natural amphitheatre-style seating, allowing for breathtaking harbour views. Under the shell roofs and the massive podium are five theatres: the Concert Hall, the Opera Theatre, the Drama Theatre, the Playhouse and the Studio Theatre.

The Concert Hall is the largest performing area in the Sydney Opera House. It is used for a range of symphony concerts, chamber music, rock and jazz concerts. The huge Concert Hall is the home to the Sydney Symphony Orchestra and it seats 2,679 people. It was designed by Peter Hall and his team.

The smaller Opera Theatre is used for opera, ballet and other dance productions. The carpet is a brilliant red and the seats are constructed from silver birch plywood. It has a seating capacity of 1,547. The orchestral pit seats eighty musicians. The Opera Theatre is the Sydney performance base for Opera Australia and the Australian Ballet.

Opera is sung in the original language and surtitles are projected, but cannot be seen in all seats. The opera entertains in the summer season from January to March, and in the winter season from June to November.

The Australian Ballet dances in the summer season from mid-March to early May, and in the winter season from November to December. Dances are contemporary in origin, as well as including popular classic performances.

The Drama Theatre is used for drama and dance. The front of the stage can be lowered to create an orchestra pit for thirty-five musicians. The carpet is vivid blue and the seats are covered with a striking tangerine-wool fabric. The performing companies in the Drama Theatre are Sydney Theatre Company, Bangarra Dance Theatre, Sydney Festival, Sydney Opera House and Bell Shakespeare. The seating capacity is 544 in nineteen rows.

The Drama Theatre, the Playhouse and the Studio have shared a large foyer since 1999.

The Playhouse is one of the most intimate performance venues within the Sydney Opera House. It is used for lectures, seminars and films. The Sydney Festival, Sydney Opera House and Bell Shakespeare Company present annual programmes in the Playhouse. The seating capacity is 398 in seventeen rows. The Playhouse has red carpet and the seats are made of birch timber with dark-purple woollen upholstery.

The Studio opened in February 1999 and it has been put to a variety of uses. Originally, it was known as the Recording Hall and is the smallest and most intimate theatre in the complex. There is seating for up to 350 people, depending upon the configuration of the venue. It was designed by Leif Kristensen and cost $7.5 million. The Studio has red carpet and a major motif of wood finishings. It is used for contemporary music, comedy and seminars.

The Sydney Opera House is the centre of high culture in Sydney and although evening wear is not required, it is one of the places where you are likely to see locals in formal attire.